T0106085

The LEADER Within

The LEADER Within

Powerful Leadership Manual

LOEL CHARLES

AuthorHouse™ LLC
1663 Liberty Drive
Bloomington, IN 47403
www.authorhouse.com
Phone: 1-800-839-8640

Published by AuthorHouse 10/17/2013

ISBN: 978-1-4918-1538-0 (sc)
ISBN: 978-1-4918-1539-7 (e)

Library of Congress Control Number: 2013916626

The Leader Within, The Inner Positive Self

This is an Upper and Upward Productions Project with Crystallized host and writer and author Loel Charles. Hello world and listening audience. I'm delighted, and I look forward to sharing my topic with you: The Leader Within. My chief and primary objective, and aim in producing this body of work, is to do something as oppose to doing nothing. With a desired interest of producing a benefit for human beings, with an overflow of happiness, and reducing a reduction in the area of human hurt and pain. Have you ever risen from sleep in the morning feeling like it's a great day? Only inconvenience by a life choice, and this life choice is the essence of wrong thinking. Consider what I mean! The thought of going through today, as if it was yesterday or yesteryear, and living that same old repetitive life cycle. Compounded by frustration, stress, rejection, emptiness, poverty, the moral break down of man to man, the wrong occupation, fear of success, or lack of success, domestic violence, abandonment, and the spirit of desperation, and procrastination. In short, the list is infinite. In the area of human existence we are one. We are a family of the conditions of life.

Let's collectively as individuals assess our life. Starting with asking ourselves what's wrong and what's right in my life, and what causes me the most grief and pain? We are going to self-inventory, and self-reflect the inner self. Buckle up and come along, and let's go inward, and take a mental journey. However, it's imperative to do this from a perspective of pure honesty, because the truth, and the essence of the truth will set us free. And this includes the freedom from: negative thinking, defeatist thoughts, and defeatist thought patterns which mean us no good. Our aim is to renew the mind and spirit, and enhance the quality of our life. Therefore, we must begin this process with the inner working of the mind. It has been said, a house built on a weak foundation will not withstand, but yet the house built on solid ground shall not wither. Therefore, we must come to a decision and conclusion. The conclusion of overcoming negative thinking, and negative thought patterns, and installing a positive thinking model in their place. I am talking about a sound mind. This model will replicate and parallel the foundation of a house built on solid ground will not wither. Replicated success.

At this point of the decision making process, we have already empowered the mind by taking an active mental stance. From this mental and altered state of mind, let's put our life into segmentation categories. This will include three categories: I will call them categories, A, B, and C.

Beginning with category (A). This is the stage of reforming the mind, or the mental born again process. This is the cleaning of the mind. We fine tune the mind, and remove the spirit of negative thinking. We do this the same way you would eat an elephant, one bite at a time. Then over a period of time, and after enough bites the elephant will dissipate and dissolve. Positively speaking we will workout the negative conditions that have been rooted in our mind, thought by thought, and over a period of time they will dissipate. Moving along to category (B). The me I Love. Because we love our self, this is the reason we have taken an active stance, and started this inward journey. This is the component that has directed us to this inward path. This is a critical stage because it empowers us inwardly, and psychologically. Moreover, it feeds and sends the sub-consciousness mind neurons with the message

I love me. This also delivers the message to the psyche I have value. We are psychological creatures by nature. Therefore, the mind must be sent the message it is loved, and this understanding begins with self. Next (C). The me I am striding to become. A happy self-functioning, self-actualized, self-individuated and happy person.

Upon troubleshooting and a thorough examination of ourselves, let's refuse to merely change. The mere changing could be going from bad to worst. Our commitment is to become improve with an overall objective of being better. Therefore, make this declaration and proclamation, and say it like you mean it, and mean it when you say it. I possess the ability and soundness of mind to overcome the strong hold of negative thinking. It has meant me no good and it means me no good, so I will not champion its cause. Instead, I will pursue the desired goals of inner peace and happiness. Hence, from this moment forward, I will reduce my thoughts of negative thinking, and negative images from hurtful moments, and less desirable experiences of the past. I have chosen to take the honest road, and the path of fair dealings in life. This act of fairness will be applied into my daily thinking, and embedded into my psyche. Therefore with this presence of mind, no experience in life is worthy of cheating me, or robbing me of happiness. In life storms will come and go, and tough times will come and go, but nothing is constant, or eternal or everlasting.

From this perspective of self, we will exam and view the underlining causes, and become as the Social Sciences would term analytical. For starters, how was our personality form? Who or how were we introduced to this code of conduct, and way of thinking, or behavior pattern that has robbed us of life? Go directly to the origin, and the root core, and not the second in command. We are going where we can get results. Now that we are here, lets deal with it. If there is a discrepancy, or you dislike the root, repair or rectify it.

Tell the root, it's my life and by the power vested in me, I'm coming to get, and reclaim my life. You have had your chance! Now say your name, I Ms. Self-Worthy, this gives your cause specific meaning, and it's an oath with yourself. I Ms. Self-Worthy, having a clear conscious, and being of independent will, and sound mind, exercise my given, and natural right, to no longer do your negative aim, or negative will, of demoralizing and diminishing my spirit. I will no longer be an active agent that will carry out your mission. In fact, I quit and your term is expired. You have manifested in the forms of psychological violence, drugs, procrastination, negligence, addiction, abusive, and massive self-afflicted behavior. Enough is enough.

In coming face to face with this truth, and the essence of our being, yes this takes courage, but this is a character trait that is innate in us. So as we inwardly arrive at the essence of our being, this is a new beginning.

Bye! Bye! Yesterday, and hello Today. I am looking forward to my new beginning. From this moment, and forward, renounce every evil ill, every self-destructive behavior, and embrace and activate the spirit of TLWI. In expanding our world view, and growth in the concept of social conditioning, and learn behavior this exposure leads to an awakening. Here is where we exit one stage of life, to enter and encounter new avenues. These avenues of heighten horizons, have led us to a more enlighten awareness of our personality development, and the modification of our personality adjustment. The modification of our mindset has led to a new and heighten understanding. This heighten understanding has transcended our previous life experiences, and has untied us in connection with our purer inner self. Having made this connection leads to a new awareness based on self-love. This broaden perspective of self-love propels and ignites us to take action, and be responsible, and apply the principles of forgiveness. It begins with the forgiven of self, and extends to all of humanity, because we all are one.

Operating from this consciousness of mind, we are open to the vastness and beauty of life. What I refer to as the Genesis of Life, and Developing the Mindset. With an open, sincere, conscious, and free mind, install the foundation of: The Leader Within, and govern yourself.

In retrospect, this process has been engaged and completed. At this point, let's return to the valley of decision. The decision stages A, B, and

C. It's time to eliminate category A. Having an expanded view and a higher level of understanding category A. The me that must reform is a person of the past, and gone for good. Because change without growth is impossible.

Galvanized with a transformation of mind we are more advanced in our thinking. Consequently we've altered our consciousness, broaden our horizon, and boosted our morale. Welcome to the Fraternity of the Living, and the Community of Life. With a born again spirit, we can chose life, live life, and be at inner peace. Never again do we have to be driven by the guide of wrongful thinking. In this mode of self-awareness, never again will we undertake in affairs that are counterproductive, and that will not enhance our mental and psychological wellbeing. Therefore, our surrounding will be supportive, energy giving and energy receiving undertakings. They will be rich in scope that encourage us and engage us and inspire us. We will embrace encounters that generate mutual positive affairs of win/win. Moving along to category, (B). The me I love, based on love and a renewal genesis and transformation that radiates inner peace. At the core of this metaphysics, is truth, honesty, righteous, and love. At minimal this is the life expectancy of our self. This is what we will encompass, and embrace. Healthy mutual relationships. Never, expect out of others, what you do not expect out of yourself. Expect the Law of Reciprocity. Last, but equally important category (C). The me I am striding to become. Be honest and give an honest testimony; confess: life is relentless and persistent if nothing else, and we are always people in process. This is why we have expanded, grown, and heighten our status throughout this sojourn. Life is a continual self discovery journey and evolution process.

It is time to lead by example, take action, and commit to growth and development with absolutely no desire for recidivism. It is time to get started, because it's always time to get started in the right direction. But it all starts inside first, so come on with a determine and made up mind.

The soul, spirit and highness of life! Do not drop out of life. Get involved in life, and be an active agent. Engage in reality thinking, and embrace the Alpha and Omega, and the Yen and Yang of life. That is from beginning to the end, and from birth to death we are surrounded, and constantly affected by polarities, and variables of life. For example, debt, hard times, loss of employment, or lack of employment, bankruptcy, losing a love one, diseases, babies born deform, mental illness, poverty, broken homes, wayward souls, violence and youth issues, health issues, betrayal, and aides, these categories, and more, all equate to life and the conditions of life. It is not mystery science, so do not harbor the negative thinking when such life encounters happen to you, and believe the false premise this is unfair treatment, because none of us are solo victims in life. In variably, prepare for the conditions of life. So we can take the bitter with the sweet, and the pleasant with the unpleasant.

Our objective is to be balance equilibriumly and well-adjusted psychologically. Knowing in our hearts and minds, anything can happen anytime to anyone, and there is no exception to the rule. It's a universal fact, all of us will be touch and move by life, both literally and figurative. Given this data, do not personalize it. Except the reality of life: Life does not single us out, and rain on our parade, summon and doom us to havoc and put us on an only island. For this I am sure. Life happens to both male and female alike; it is not a gender thing. Life is in the business of equal opportunity. When we accept the reality and conditions of life, we understand we can be our own worst enemy, or our own best friend. It is as simple as that. We have a choice, and this choice is ours to make. We can be lead by negative thinking or positive thinking. This is the foundation of TLWI.

Often we rely on rationalized width, but to no avail. Frequently we conclude the false perception: Life Isn't Fair. False, False, False and more False. This is an erroneous premise and weak argument. This allows us to rationalize, and justify our disdain for our life circumstance and condition. Then we lay this weak foundation down to justify our efforts for being mediocre. However, relevantly and factually speaking, life is as fair as it gets. In fact, life is more than fair. Life is extremely fair. Life does not care about class status, geographical, social, political, economic status, religious point of view, genetics, stature, race or creed. Rich person, poor person, atheist, believer, agnostic, people of humanity, and people in general. We are all missionaries of the movement of life.

The Bible says it rains on the just and unjust alike, and the sun shines on the just and unjust alike. This is fair application of life. This means men, women, elderly and children alike. Therefore, when the elements of life subpoena us do not scorn with the notion, you are being unjustly lash. Accept the conditions that will be presented to you, and rise up and wise up, and refuse to be weighted down. It is imperative to change the way we think with sound information, because then we change the condition, and quality of our life, for the good and the better. In this spirit, we will enhance and manifest an upgraded lifestyle. When we clean our mind, we clean our thoughts, so our verbal is purified and edified as well. Therefore if we are what we mentally eat, we will not practice in self-defeatist thinking. Do not allow such phrases to come out of your mouth, if it was not for bad luck, I would not have any luck, I just can't win, I will never be able to do that, Some people get all the breaks, Life is not fair. This is self-defeatist talk, and mental conditions of mind. To the contrary with the new thought process in our thinking, and thought process of our mind, there should be phrases and beliefs as: I am doing the best I know how, and when I learn better, I am going to do better, I am capable of handling any life experience, I cannot be beat, I will not be beat, I was born to win, and I refuse to lose, I will never be beat, I can handle anything life puts in my path. Implement this positive thinking into your daily life, and foster this belief. Then replace all negative thoughts, with positive ones, and focus on doing better. Reconstruct your life and be guided by TLWI, and look at LIFE as an acronym that translates to: Life Is Fair Everyone! Every time that negative inner self rises to the surface, kill that spirit, and refuse to compromise. We have to monitor the way we think, and what enters into our mind, and how we choose to filter and process that information. In a like manner, we must monitor the verbal that comes out of our mouth. It is imperative to have a positive and healthy state of mind. A direct correlation of mental and verbal relationship.

Today and henceforth, I am an empowered and positive thinker in my approach to life. I will refuse to get sick, and I reject any disease. I will refuse to get old, because old is a state of mind, compared to where aging is a natural process of living, and maturing. Think of how many times we have witness senior citizens paving the way for the youth movement in terms of active living. Bright and early they are up at dawn. They are walking, running, jogging, exercising, reading, camping, fishing and full of life. Essentially they are displaying the love and quest for life. They are radiant, upbeat, and their minds are active, fresh, and sharp. They are constantly on the move, and consistently doing something of a positive nature, and challenging life to the fullest. These mature people refuse to get old. I can recall the story of a 75 year old man and grandfather who was gearing up to swim across an ocean, which was known to have sharks. This did not matter. He was actively doing something, and pursing a personal goal. Rather he made it, or not is not the point. The point is he refused to be limited by the spirit of negative thinking to use his age as a handicapped, to not pursue a meaningful, and personal goal. Just think about the message he sent his grandchildren. Another man in his 90's graduated from college, after having started college in his youth, but not finishing it due to time served in the military, as a result of being drafted. Later in life and in his 90's, he fulfilled his educational goal and graduated, and received his bachelor degree. This 90 year man, like the 75 year old grandfather, refused to use his age as a handicap. In essence, when we engage in negative thinking, we place artificial barriers, and limits on our personal goals. Some of us are under the age of 40, and have conceded to the notion, of being over the hill, and peaked out in life. Well, I flunked out of that school, and invite all others to do the same. In fact, it is time to get better with age. I am talking about the age of our beginning to the eternity of living. Do not blame life for being life. Everything in the universe has its purpose, and life is no different. Respect, honor, and cherish life and life's functions. Develop and work with what has been instilled and entrusted in you. Then manifest it, and align it in accordance to your life's purpose.

Do not measure success by where you are, but measure it by where you are, in reference to where you are from. I believe this is worth mentioning again. Do not measure success by where you are, but measure it by where you are, in reference to where you are from. No one size fits all, because no two people are the same. Therefore the measurement of success is not the same for everyone. I call this: ISA, Individualized Success Awareness.

Case and Point: During my tenure as a college student my former instructor was giving a lecture on success. In which he cited a scenario which consisted of two of his former students. One a C student, who won student of the year award for most outstanding student. The other student was an honor's student with an A average. As the results for most outstanding student were announced, the honor's student lamented, "I made all A's, what about me?" The instructor tactfully responded. You have been an honor's student from day one, with little or no effort. The C student with perseverance, tenacity, and a desire to succeed raised his letter grade from failing to a C average. The best letter grade improvement he had witness over his twenty year tenure. Both students were successful, but from different perspectives.

Eliminate bad day thinking. There are good days, better days, and even better days. Practice the art of being happy every day, and start your day with positive thinking. Upon rising in the morning build the foundation of your day with positive thoughts and thinking. Invest 20 minutes into your day, starting when you wake up to think positive. Start by mediating and having a peaceful mindset. Then focus on positive images, and good and positive things that will happen for you, and to you during the day, and throughout the day. Tell yourself today is going to be a great day, I will have a productive, and harmonious day, and I will draw and attract positives sources into my life. Incorporate this method of self-healing, and life enrichment in your life, for the enhancement, and liberation of the mind. Refuse, absolutely refuse to start your day without positive reflection. In business each day, there is a goal on how the business is projected to begin, and the objective for the day, and it will not have a business plan that is not positive. We must daily plan our life with positive thinking, in the same model and project positive dividends. Model Success!

Each day is a rewarding day, and presents the opportunity for advancement, achievement, and growth. Have a daily goal every day. It could range from being a better parent, sister, brother, teacher, neighbor, advocate, economist, or anything positive and meaningful. There is no limit to your goal, only you can decide its depth. One of my daily goals is to grow in self-awareness, and increase my self-worth, and self-value, and make a contribution to the family of life. Additionally, I want to grow in knowledge each day. Therefore, I am in constant engagement and evolution in life. My slogan is: I'll be better before I'll be worst, and here is an open invitation to each and every person with no exception. However, this may require an alternative course and flexible approach. I wish I could give the solemn promise that there would be pleasure without pain, but life is not that kind of companion. Life pushes us around sometimes and can be overwhelming, and have bully like tendencies. But we have to stand right back up to life, and stand up for ourself. We have to challenge life back, and tell life thank you, and I am not intimidated by you. I am a fighter, so that mean, I am going to fight back. I have mental training for you, and I have prepared for you. I know I will get some bumps and bruises, but I will heal. In the end, my pains will allow me to be stronger, better, and wiser. I thank you for the role you will play in my achievement, advancement and success, so I accept the life experience with the understanding what doesn't kill me, makes me stronger and wiser. Moreover, I will not take it personal, because I understand this is your purpose, and nature. In fact, when you operate on this level of awareness with an expanded consciousness, you understand it all has been due to direct encounters, from the trials and tribulations directly associated with life, which have made us the steadfast people we are, or the steadfast people we are in the process of becoming.

In knowing how to live, we can find the life of the party in every situation, so if we cannot change the situation, then we have to change the way we view the situation. Develop an appetite for life, and be enthusiastic, carefree, creative, and charismatic. Feel good because we deserve happiness. So have charisma in life. There is a proverbial teaching that teaches, "If I'm not for myself who is for me?" So let the journey, the long awaited journey begin. So when someone asks, why are you so happy? Tell them practice, practice, and more practice. How does any champion, or top professional get to the top? Practice, Practice, and more Practice. Practice pays off in all things, and it is no different with being happy. If you want to be happy think and practice happy thinking. It will, and it has to pay off.

There will be the moments in life where we will need to grief, lament, regroup, and cry. This is okay, and in fact, this is completely healthy, and part of the process to be whole. Allow yourself time to overcome devastation and hardships. Hardships are a natural process of life, but the race does not belong to the swift, but to those who endure.

Take an athlete for example, regardless of how gifted they are, they must prepare and train for their event. If they do not, than they will not master their craft and skill. Therefore, when it is time for their event, or their performance, it will speak to the level of their training, and mental mindset. No matter how gifted they are, they will not get their maximum, or peak performance for their event. This means they will perform to the level of their training, both mental and psychical. So during critical moments of their event, their skill level will be exploited due to lack of preparation. This holds true in the arena of life as well. During critical moments of life, if we have not prepared our minds for critical moments, or engaged in positive thinking for critical moments, than life will cobble us up. We become prey to life. Failing to prepare, is preparing to fail. Positive mental exercise couple with the proper mental frame of reference, allow us to be at our peak mentally. Moving along, we must implement the 5 P's of preparation with our positive mental mindset. Positive Proper Psychological Preparation Plan. Therefore, we must continually engage in the manner of daily implementation of the schema of TLWI. So in preparing our mind for the hardships of life, we put ourselves at minimum risk for the psychological challenges that are bonded to life.

We must sharpen our mental capacities to think critical. In higher order of thinking, think in the terms of worst case scenario, modern scenario, and mild scenario. Then we visualize having an emotional plan, and action plan, that will enable us to make positive choices. In these critical and challenging moments of life. Through visualization we see ourselves enduring and overcoming the situation, and we see ourself handling it in a positive way. In fact, in this sphere of thinking is: Except the worst, except the best, and anything in between. This scope is broad, but indeed such is life. During this visualization process it reveals cognitive and blatant realization, that we are one situation from better or worse, or richer or poorer. The task at hand is to be bold, brave, determined, strong willed, enduring, and flexible. All of these adjectives and attributes will be skills needed for the journey of happy and peaceful living.

Adjust to anything life offers. Then elevate and get your coping skills up to par, because there is not a problem that cannot be fix. Our coping skills allow us to develop a keenness for hope, and where there is hope, there is life and where there is life, there are possibilities. Throughout human history, people from all walks of life, have endured and overcome the most dare of realities, and most difficult circumstances. This is a history to embrace, and replicate.

There is not a person that is a product of a man and woman that is not a child of life. Therefore there is a direct correlation that is connected to the bitterness and setbacks of life, that is tied into overcoming, such challenges with fortitude. Because freedom is not free. To attain any level of happiness in life, we must endure, and prevail, and this is part of the equation. We cannot disconnect, so we must embrace this fact. The diversity of life is rich in the character of hardship. Many of us can relate to the diversity of hardship. Throughout human history people have overcome crippling, harsh, and extreme circumstances. People like you and I. This is human history worthy of tapping into.

I marvel when I think of the various forms of adversity people have face and overcome. The biographies and stories I have read about, and listen to on audio, and taken in psychology, sociology, and counseling classes, and heard in lectures, and training classes, and of people I have encountered in my personal life. These stories of people mastering seemingly hopeless conditions and adversity, which I have stored and locked in my memory. Sources from all avenues of life: Heads of state that have overcome conditions of childhood where they never knew a parent or they had to overcome a background of an alcoholic parent. Moses the liberator in the bible had to overcome slur of speech to lead a nation of people, a top rated celebrity who had been fired over twenty times, think about all of that rejection, but rose the ranks and became an industry leader. I have heard some top orators and business leaders account for things they endured and encountered, and overcame. Some of the stories were how they had abusive parents, and some never knew their parents, one told the struggle of finishing two grades behind in high school, and being label mentally retarded. Think about all of the teasing and negative images this person had to be subjected to, and endured, but still this person rose above these challenged conditions to become a master, and top rated industry leader in their area of public demand, and also won various prominent awards. Another story that echo in my ears is of a rape victim and homeless run away youth and teen parent, but was still able to overcome these emotional wounds and life mishaps, and write many books, and also able to speak around the world, and connect with nations, and millions of people. This person had become a top notch author, and television personality. I can recall reading how one of the nation's richest men did not get his start to wealth until in his 40's, and he was not born into wealth. Stories of how several people had dropped out of high school, and did not complete college, but they had found ways to become billionaire's. I have seen where people have gone to prison and get reformed and become administrators within the same prison they served time in. Still, others that were in prison discovered their inner self and other side and went on to write and publish best selling novels. I recall reading a pamphlet of a person who was the state head, and the top official at the divisional level give testimony of how at one time she had served time in prison, and despite of that, she was able to reconstruct her life, and work her way up to the head of the administration, and become the department head. I can recall where several musical artists had been told they lack talent, and would never make it. Yet, they were able to rise above the experts' opinions and sell millions of records, and make it to the top of the music industry, and star in several highly acclaim movies as well. In sports there are the stories of players not given up on themselves when they are not drafted, and then when they are cut by several teams, and are not wanted by any professional team. But they never give up on themselves, and despite the odds they overcome them. They remain positive and keep believing in themselves and their abilities. Then one day, not only have they made the team, but they become hall of famers, and future hall of famers. I once read a story and watched a movie about how a person that was born with down syndrome was counted out at birth by doctors. His parents were told to put him into an institution. The doctors had counted him out and thought this was best for him. However, this child overcome the negative stigma and went on to star in several movies. Just think about that positive impact. I recall watching a program about a child with autism who was an artist, and how the child was able to draw exceptionally well. His paintings were breath taking, and when the commentator asked him how was he able to paint so well? the child responded, "because I am smart." He was very positive. Further I recall reading one of the best selling books on self help, riches and personal growth, where the author shared how his son was born into the world without ears and how he was told by the doctors he would never be able to hear, and to except this as a reality of life. The author rejected this notion, and told the doctor such. And as the author proclaimed his son was able to gain 100 percent of his hearing. And his son went on to work for an acoustic company and help many others to hear that faced the same or similar problem. Tough times, and hard times, and overcoming them are not new sciences in life. Therefore, regardless of how troubling a situation may appear to be, envision yourself having inner drive and inner believe of TLWI, and faith thinking, to not be denied. In life we are one.

United we stand, and together we are bonded and connected to the conditions of life. Therefore we all have a direct correlation, and direct link that ties into tribulation, sorrow, hurt and pain, trial and error, but nothing in life is eternal, or endless. Struggle is ordain and prepares us for life, and greatness. Our origin is one.

There is a simplistic yet profound story about a man that was introduced to belief one day. The story was of a poor man having a life time, of hard times, bad luck, calamity, and all manner of misfortunate. This man believed this was his destiny for eternity. However, one day he went to see a fortune teller. The fortune teller read his hand, and looked into his future, and projected great things for him. This included wealth and happiness, and some of the finest comfort life had to offer. As time had passed, and like the forecast of the fortune teller had projected, he had accrued wealth, greatness, and an abundance of royalties in life. Being ecstatic and overflowing with joy he decided to revisit the fortune teller with the news. Ms. Fortune Teller like you prophesied and predicted, I've acquired wealth, happiness, and abundance in life. The fortune teller paused, and then responded, I'm so happy and delighted, but the truth of the matter is 'I'm not a fortune teller. I just wanted to introduce you to belief. The belief of yourself. Laugh! Laugh! Laugh! The Power of One.

How many of us are like this man and think self-defeatist thoughts, and get what we think? I will call this the self-fulfilling prophecy syndrome. Well, let's relinquish this way of thinking and uproot it from our repertoire of mental thinking, and make it a composite of the past.

Because this way of thinking is a dream killer, and spirit killer. It cripples and enables us, and promotes mediocrity and procrastination. However the thinking of positive thinking propels us to higher heights. Therefore, incorporate a believe system with the premise of positive thinking, that will magnify and enrich the mind, and manifest a utopia way of living. Regard the mind as a computer chip that needs to be program, and you being the programmer. Therefore, we can design a program to our liken and choosing. Simple we choose our own program. Consequently this program will respond to our directives: Garbage in Garbage out, Beauty in Beauty out, Success in Success out. In essence we will program our mind to be negative or positive. We are the programmers of our thinking, so let's instill and install positive thinking as our model. There is a direct correlation between belief and success. It is nothing mystical, the principles of positive thinking have been around since ancient history. We see it every day. In the direct correlation of the sun, moon, and stars in regards to them submitting to the positive principles of the universe. I can recall a story from childhood about a toy train that had a strong and positive will to succeed. This train was having some challenges of completing its course on the track, and was about to stop, but it energized itself with the power of positive thinking: I think I can, I think I can, I think can, I know I can, and the train did it. Through the belief of positive thinking, and positive affirmations, the toy train was able to carry on, and complete the task. So when we apply the formula of positive thinking it works, and it is not complicated. Once we apply the formula and principles of positive thinking to any problem large or small, it's not as problematic. But there is an order to things, so first things first. The prerequisite and criteria is to pay our dues in life, and no one gets the luxury of being exempt. Remember life was not incorporated in this manner. Even the beasts, fowls, rodents, and the creatures of marine life follow this rational. The best things in life are earn, and learn, not free. This is one of life's most fundamental rules. One has to give something to get something on every level of life. It goes back to having the power of choice. So when you exam the price tag that applies to your circumstance, or situation, then also know there is a sacrifice, or requirement that's affixed to the situation. What is the price or maximum effort are you willing to invest in yourself and of yourself, and out of yourself for a rewarding upgraded and enriched life? There is a proverbial saying that states: if its to be its up to me. Are you willing to admit, maybe yesterday's teachings are today's lessons? Are you willing to adapt a different ideology, or make sacrifices? How much human capital are you willing to bring into your circle? Are you willing to change the people and places, and things you have bonded with? Are you ready for a new venue, or a new perspective? Are you ready to disconnect and disassociate with support systems that have been counterproductive in scope? Are you willing to hit rock bottom? Are you sick and tired of being sick and tired? As the sales person would ask, what is your bottom line or bottom dollar? These are questions and a series of thoughts to nourish and ponder on, as food for thought. Physician heal thy self.

Be strong, courageous, bold, wise, understanding, knowledgeable, fearless and positive. Have strength and courage to try, and keep trying, but yet flexible enough to change. Because in life, we can plan one way and things can go the other way. So we have to be flexible to adjust to the flexibility of life. This means we have to have a backup plan, and a backup, backup plan. I will acknowledge it can be frustrating, discouraging, and frankly speaking: it can be exhausting and overwhelming. However, our mind of positive thinking has prepared us for this. At times, we will need to step back, and away from the problem, and relax and do not over exert negative energy. Therefore do not despair, or be rattled. Take a break away from the encounter, and then see yourself being emotionally mature, and flexible, and in a positive frame of mind. Then see yourself addressing the encounter. I think I can, I think I can, I think I can, I know I can, and do it. Put together a life plan, and succeed. Combat every negative thought that surface, and do not let it take root in the mind. Revert to your positive mental training and positive thinking, and to TLWI, and purify the inner self with healing spirits. The healing spirits of peace, joy, and happiness. The healing spirits of positive thinking. Oh! Doesn't it feel self-gratifying and enhancing and empowering to harness an entitlement of freedom without the hindrance of negative thinking? This is an empowering power that resonates to the inner soul.

Desire to be in charge of your life, and your life's choices. Because all of our choices will impact the reality of our existence. Keep desire alive, because desire motivates us and challenges us and propel us to be whole. Desire is a strong motivation. My personal desire is I have always wanted to be the best in the world at something, and help others in the process. However, wanting to do something is not good enough. Ask any cognitive person if they want to do something of value, or importance in life, and it will be a unanimous yes. Having goals are awesome, but that is not enough. Once we have a shift in thinking, and an improved understanding, we will understand goals are essential, but they are just a component of the process. Therefore it is going to take a commitment, coupled with a course of action, and a concerted effort from TLWI. Now we can let the new and develop inner self and TLWI manifest and soar to higher horizons. Unleash its creativeness, and greatness and unlimited potential.

The importance of having goals. Goals are like missing pieces to a beautiful puzzle. Without the missing pieces to the puzzle, we would never get the vastness and beauty of the puzzle. In having goals this is a tremendous aim and step in the right direction, but this will not be enough. Goals point us in the direction we want to go, and they give us a degree of focus, but they can only carry us so far. Therefore, we will need an expectancy of our self. Okay so let's put all of the pieces together, and make this an extraordinarily beautiful puzzle. Maybe that means reading several books to an infinite amount, relocating, cutting ties with current associates, enrolling in college, working two or three jobs, getting a life coach, a counselor, a mentor, connecting with support groups, starting over, transforming your worldview, and mentally being made over, replace old knowledge and information with new knowledge and new information, making changes, improvising, being imaginative or creative, tapping inside of the inner self, and calling upon the universe for direction, help, support, and guidance.

Life helps those that help themselves: For instance, I was a poor student in grade school, middle school and high school. Further I was economically disadvantaged with no income, or preparation, or desire for academic interest in college, or trade school. I had completed high school two grades behind, and with a low C average, and number 67 out of 90 in my graduating class. Therefore shortly after graduating from high school, and being ambitious and desperate at the same time, and wanting an improved life for myself, I moved from the state of Texas to the state of Arizona, with only two hundred dollars. This was all it took. An act of me wanting to help myself. It was like the power of one act, set off a chain reaction for the universe to come to my aide. It started in my mind. In the core of my mind was positive thinking: I wanted better for myself, and the universe provided the rest. I moved to another state with my poor education, and no work skills of my past history, but wanted a better life despite the limiting, and impoverish hand I was dealt, but when I took this act of boldness, which was really an act of faith, I did not have a clue on how my life was going to evolve. I was moving with the notion of trying something different, and knowing I wanted better out of life. After relocation, and as sometime had lapsed, in this new state, I met a person that convinced me to go to trade school. I had no interest in trade school; however, I went and finished. This was my first degree, which was an Associates. Next, the value of reading was brought to me, by what I call an angel. This person instilled in me the importance of reading, and shared with me, this is how you broaden your vocabulary, and worldview. In short, upgrading my mind, and a mental makeover. Further, I was told this is how you are able to communicate on a mass level. This information empowered me to transform my life, for the good and better. Never before had I understood the value of reading, and its importance. Once I understood the value of reading it set my life on a new and different course forever. Reading had become and remains my companion, and it inspired me to take action in all areas of my life, including expanding my academic awareness. So I began taking classes for self-improvement sake. Never with a desire to get a degree. I only wanted to take classes of self-interest, which I enjoyed. All along the classes were stimulating and fun, but not challenging because now, my understanding and mindset was different. I was able to make association with the content, based on my new love for reading, and the subjects I was taking, I could tie them into what I had read. I did not realize this was having a working knowledge of content matter, and prior background knowledge. Additionally, the classes I was taking were as affordable as $5.00 per semester credit unit, or an unlimited amount of classes with a cap of $50.00. So not only were the classes stimulating and fun, but they were very economical. Remember I said life helps those that help themselves. Unbeknownst to me the foundation was been laid for me to get two additional college degrees, and they would come painless, and none of them would cause me any hardships. In addition, I found myself being a tutor to other students. I was like the child born with out ears that was able to hear, and went back to help others that was like him to overcome their battle with hearing. I was able to help struggling students. All of this as a result of making a mind shift from negative to positive thinking. The blessing of the Lord maketh one rich and causes no sorrow. I never ask for a degree, and I never wanted a degree, but because my heart desired learning, I learned, and learned, and I increased my learning. I would take a course one at a time, two at a time, and at times I would stop going to college. But I would always read and keep my learning going. I would move from one state to another state seeking advancement opportunity, but my self-improvement through reading was a constant at all times. I would read 3 or 4 different books at a time, and they would be wide in scope. I would read on business subjects, topics in economics, sociology, mythology, philosophy, psychology, religion, anthropology, humanities, history, english and writing, and self-help. My interest and motive was for self-improvement and the acquisition of knowledge solely. I followed this format for twelve years, of on and off, of taking classes. It has been said you eat an elephant one bite at a time, so I ate the elephant one bite at a time. Over a period of time the elephant dissipated.

The Power of One. I heard one radio announcement enroll in the local community college and your first class is free. I love improving myself so I did just that, and my second degree was given to me as such. I was taking a break from a class, and I met another student who was also on break, and who I will call an angel that propelled me to act. We were talking on break and I was asked what my major was? I responded I did not have one, and I was only taking classes for self-improvement. This conversation led to my sharing of my educational background. As a result of me sharing my educational background this angel responded: you have taken enough classes for an associate degree. To this day I would have not known, I had already completed enough classes for a second associate degree. I went and talked with a counselor, and as this angel had proclaimed, I had taken enough classes for an associate. I was only a few classes short. The amazing part was it was already paid for, and I had already taken enough classes for a certificate, which was also already paid for. I received my associate and graduated with high honors and among the elite with my GPA. In graduating in elite status, I was also able to attain a personal goal of being the best at something, like I had always envision of myself, and in the same process, I had help tutor other students, so I was also able to help others which is something I had always envision. So, I attained two goals in one, and I was rewarded for my efforts. Just like that, I had two degrees, and neither one had I wanted, or planned for, and they both were paid for. I stop attending college after graduating, but like before I continued my learning, by way of reading, which consisted of a variety of subjects, and three and four books at a time. Following this same pattern, about three years later I met another angel, and who was a college student, and we were having a conversation about a book I had read, and one she was reading in her class. Based on my knowledge of the subject, she was wooed by my intellect. Therefore, my college background came up again, like before in the conversation of some previous years before in another state, that took place on the college campus with the other angel. I mentioned to her what my educational background was. Like before, I was told I was close to a having a Bachelor Degree, and like before I did not know it. Once more, here was an angel placed into my life to deliver me a message that I should go and talk with a counselor at the university. And just like before, I did just that, and like before this angel was right. The counselor told me, I was only 11 classes short of a Bachelor degree in Liberal Arts, and I had no idea, or clue, what Liberal Arts was. When it was explained to me, I did not know until I wrote this book, it was something I had been doing my entire life, since I had acquired the love for reading. It was a degree that is broad in scope, and for a person that has a wide range of interest. They are design for writers, educators, business professions, and people who like to think. The counselor told me since I had took so many courses in the social sciences field, and sociology, and psychology, and human services my degree easily could be a human service degree. I was just happy to hear I was so close to a Bachelor Degree, that I never had planned for, or that never was a goal of mine, that I missed the connection, it was in a related area of interest of mine. Writing, Human Services, Education, and People centered. It addressed every area of my interest, and it was broad like my reading. Life helps those that help themselves. Again like in all trends of my acquired education, the cost to me was minimum. I was working for an employer that incurred a bulk of the cost. I took the classes and like before none were challenging, I finished with a perfect 4.00, and graduated in elite status with my bachelor. My 3rd degree, also I accomplished my personal goal of being the best at something again by graduating with a 4.00. I was among the very best at something, and likewise, I also was a note taker for students with disabilities. So again, I was able to help others in the process. I now had 3 degrees that I never planned for or wanted, and all were paid for. I had transformed my low and poor status from my youth and adolescence to graduating with an associate and bachelor degree with high honors. All by changing my mindset, and having installed TLWI. In leading up to this process it followed a common theme of the Power of One: In one state I meet one person that encouraged me to get an associates from a trade school. Then I meet one person that introduces me to the importance of reading. I move to another state and I hear one message about one free class. From here, I met one person that tells me I have enough classes to get an associate from the community college. Next, I move to another state, and I meet one person which tells me: I have taken enough classes to be close to having a bachelor. It was as if, once I reached out for help, a map and course was aligned, and my steps and actions were directed, and there were people and money waiting there to aid me. The Power of One and Life helps those that help themselves.

Once I discovered the impact of social conditioning and the seeds of purpose along with being rooted in TLWI. I was able to resurrect my doormat abilities, to the opposite extreme. I went from being a very poor student to one of the best students. Was it easy, at first not at all, I had to redirect my mindset from negative to positive, and couple this into tangible action of self-discipline, recreational reading, traveling, meeting and confiding in people from all walks of life, taking risk, making mistakes but learning from them. In retrospect, they were opportunities to expand my knowledge base, and without doubt I had to transform my mind. Yes, I had to be born again and inner directed by TLWI.

The mind is psychological in scope and it is amazing once we go inward and galvanize it with positive thinking, how this inward path has a positive mental effect that acts as a sinusoidal wave, and positive ripple, that generates a positive mental effect, which has a polarizing and positive trickledown effect. Being guided by TLWI has empowered my life in other areas: For one, I was diagnosed as a type 2 diabetic in 1999. At one time it was the third leading cause of death in the United States, but never was I intimidate by it's bullying tendencies. With my mental training for life, and implementation of TLWI, I have been able to curtail this affliction without any medicine. In fact, my medicine has been knowledge, exercise, diet, and faith that I will, and can beat this condition of life. Truly, this has been one of the best blessings in my life, it has allowed me to take control in an area that I was neglecting, and in the process let me gain more belief and confidence in the power of positive thinking. For the record, it has assured me taking charge of my life is a liberating feeling. Consequently, the ultimate compliment was when the doctor said let me shake your hand, this is amazing, you mean to tell me you were able to bring your sugar levels under control without the aid of medicine. I wish all of my patients were like you. (The truth of the matter is they all are). I am just an inner guided person by TLWI, with intervention and guidance from the universe. I only offer these facts as confirmation when you take action, you get action. Life helps those that help themselves. Moreover, when one is inner directed TLWI will surface, and the way will be clear. I know from experience it will guide and propel you to states and conditions of mind you would never think possible. There was the time I hired an attorney to represent me in a case, and seek $10, 000 dollars on my behalf, for damages I had accrued. But he did not get the desired result I had hoped for. He then told me he had done all he could do. I got absolutely no money. About six months later, my spirit, and mind was overtaken by an inward force, literally I was in a trance. In this state of mind, I was directed to write a letter on my own behalf, to seek the $ 10, 000 dollars, that the attorney was unable to recovery on my behalf. I am not an attorney, but I listen to my inner voice. I wrote the letter, asking for the same amount $ 10, 000 dollars. I did not get this amount either like I had asked, but instead I got double. I was allotted $20, 000 dollars. Once again, life helps those that help themselves. I was glad that the attorney did not get the $10, 000 dollars minus his fees. This lead me to understand sometime the best thing that can happen to you is the worst thing that can happen to you. Life is about discovery and self-discovery; therefore, as long as the journey leads to the knowledge of self, then consequently every encounter is an enhanced benefit. Further, there was the time I took on an employment opportunity with one of the largest employers in the state of Texas, in which I was not the most qualified applicant, but I went into the interview with the spirit of positive thinking, and the mindset I was going to get the job. I was notified within one week that I had passed the interview, and my interview score was the highest ever made in the history of the company, and I was offered the position. This was a result of positive thinking. I thought my way into the highest interview score ever, and the job. Within 8 months on the job, I received the award as the best supervisor in the company, and I had beaten out supervisors that had been with the department for over twenty years. This was directly related to me having a positive state of my mind at the onset of the job interview. Next, I was in a similar situation, I had took a different employment position in the department of education to lead an in school suspension program. This would be my first encounter with working in this realm. Like with the other employer, I went into the interview with a positive frame of mind, I told myself this job was mine. I interviewed and I was hired on the spot. My positive thinking, gave me the job on the spot, and I also was given eight years of experience to start with on top of this. So, not only did positive thinking reward me with a position I had never done before it rewarded me with 8 years of a salary increase. In addition, I was given the job with no training, but I was told to write the rules, policies and procedures for the program. Within nine months, I was told by the administration, the school had never run so well within the fifty years it had been open. All of this goes back to having a positive state of mind. Having a positive state of mind will have a trickledown effect. It was the same when I coached youth football, and basketball. I never had coached before, and did it for only three years, but every year my team went to the championship in every sport. My method of coaching was positive thinking, and this is what I instilled into the kids. Through positive coaching the kids went to three championships in football and won all three, three championships in basketball, and won two out of three. In basketball, the only loss was by one point in the championship game. All of these experiences are tied to positive thinking. Like in coaching it was like with my education I never wanted to coach or envisioned my self coaching, but I was sent an angel that asked me to do it. I agreed and in the process ended up helping the youth win 5 championships and doing something I never knew I could do. Once again, these experiences were centered around positive thinking.

It is time to start because we are on the clock, and the moment is critical. Come on and do not deny yourself. Progress is the name of the game. Lets go full pledged forward. Refuse, to let burdens or obstacles prevent you from moving forward with your life. Make the adjustments. Anything that takes the quality out of life, or prevents you from progressing change it right now. Now is the time to respond, it's in your control, and time is of the essence, so stop taking time for granted. As an active life force this is a choice that is ready, and available to be acted on at your command. Being refocus and focus allows us to live life without a limit. You, and only you can take charge of your life; it's your call. Practice this saying and belief: if it's to be it's up to me.

What is it you would like to be doing, or consider your life's mission? What would you consider your ideal life's accomplishment? Now ask yourself, what prevents me from doing it? Whatever surfaces from this self-interaction, which is nothing other than soul searching. Then respond, and act upon it. Now you have a perspective so improve and make the life adjustment. Either improvise or eliminate what is in your path. It's the same concept that is employed in businesses. If a business or business strategy is not getting the desired business projection, they analyze the business, then they make changes or they downsize. (Which is improvising). Master your circumstances by being led by TLWI. There is an ancient saying a man can conquer a thousand times a thousand men, but the man that conquers himself is the greatest of all conquers.

Think of (5) things within the realm of your abilities and talents you consider your purpose. Because the more you know about your purpose, the more you know about yourself. Now think of all the reasons, you can do them with the power of positive thinking as an accomplice, and not having cant for an option. Cant is not an option. I knew a lady that likes to debate and wanted to attend college, but did not have the means so she developed a book club, which required membership dues. This was an avenue to raise funding for her education. Upon joining, each member had to compile a list of books to read, and at the first of the month, all books had to have been read. On the first of the month also, was the day for group discussion, and sharing the knowledge of the subject, and debating. Since she was unable to attend college, she created the college atmosphere that addressed her need. Lack of economic resources wasn't an inhabitance factor at all. She simply converted a negative into a positive, and choose an alternative and productive route. This kept her mind sharp and active, so when she did attend college, her mind was already in the reading, studying and college mode.

Alternative routes are essentially having backup plans, and sometimes we need them to arrive at our destination. However we sometimes give too much perceived false value to stumbling blocks, and detours. Only to realize later, those where really signs aimed in the right direction after all. I'll always remember the story about the man rushing to get to the airport to catch a plane, but he was late and missed it, and as a result he became angry and upset. Well, that flight just so happen to crashed without any survivor; consequently, this detour saved his life. Therefore, not having an ideal situation in life, is not a reason to fold up your tent, or jump ship, or to be downtrodden. To the contrary its time to build your character. Feeling sorry for yourself and getting down in the gutter does not help you. In fact it only compounds the matter. So get yourself right back into the game of life. No, problem with being down, just don't get too comfortable being there. A winning sport's team, or championship's team may get down, but they do not get to comfortable there. They regroup, make adjustments, change the game plan, and then get right back into the game. It is no different in life. Replicated Success.

Do not get to low or too high, keep things in a balanced content, and within the range of your abilities. Know who you are, and know who you are not. In sports this is call playing within the limits of your capabilities. Then you do not hurt the team. It is the same when living our life we must not make unrealistic goals outside of our capabilities, which in turn will hurt us. Maturity requires of us to except things the way they are, and if they are less than ideal change or improve upon them. Do not feel guilty, jealous, or less than. Feel secure in the linage of human history, because we all are one. In life there are varying degrees, so we all have different talents, and are at varying degrees. Some get more, and some less. Regardless to our talents, or circumstances, it does not divorce us from the conditions of life, neither good nor bad, so we still have worth and value. Therefore we must live accordingly: little known, little required, lot known, lot required. Everyone was not born to be the Messiah, Prophet, President, King, Queen, Dignitary, Philanthropist, or Royalty. So, take delight and homage in accepting this universal fact. Knowing as individuals, we are given our own set of uniqueness. For instance, I'm delighted to have as my own: my DNA, my fingerprints, my purpose, my disposition, my destiny, my brain and thinking, and connection to life. We are uniquely equal in some manner, so be optimistic. That is the power of choice. Choice is like voting, you can cast your vote for inner peace, positive thinking, stress free living, or anything optimistic. So a word to the wise, use your vote well.

Be a doer, thinker, risk taker and get fired up. Winners know how to win. Develop an everything to win, and nothing to lose kind of attitude, and get the winning sprit. Refuse to let anything hold you back. Success is an attitude, and a winning attitude is the thing winners are made of. Having a winning attitude allows us to fail our way to the top. It all happens a little by little or one step at a time. It is a process. Throughout life we are people in process. Remember, Rome was not built in a day.

Failing at something allows us to discover what we are proficient at. It is basically a trial and error proceeding and process by elimination session. My attitude in life harbored where I made a truce with myself and the divine good. The arrangement went as follows: I submit and except, the earth is a product of labor, and work. Furthermore, I embrace as the truth, I was created in a like fashion. That is I am a product and replication of labor and work, that is patterned after the earth we encompass. Therefore, being a byproduct of this work ethic which is in the genetic fiber of my nature, I therefore, accept wholeheartedly the principles that govern labor and work. Likewise, I except if I do not work, I will not prosper, or benefit from the laws that govern earth and man alike.

The principles of work and labor are highlighted to emphasize the importance of work. When you understand and apply the principles of work, you have every entitled right to demand satisfaction and gratification in accordance to the law that govern the universe. Its like the story of the patient who lead a very active life, who become terminally ill, and who asked for a solution to the problem in the form of an ultimatum. God the patient respectfully prayed, restore and heal me to my former health, or have my life. The patient was granted favor and restored to health.

Without question, do not ask for anything without an eagerness to reciprocate equal compensation in return predicated on work. Expect nothing for free. Be an advocate for justice and balance, and a willing steward that gives an earnest effort for the pursuit of your happiness. With a willingness to work, surrender your will to the principles of work, and the principles for which they stand. Submit there is no such reality as a free lunch in life. Respectfully, understand work is a key in life, and that work starts with self. Faith without work is dead. Having this insight is imperative because we must first work with our self, and from this work will manifest a peace of mind. Yet, lack of work is like being casted into a lake of doom, and an idle mind is the devil's worship. Therefore we must summon and reap the rewards of the work ethic. While at the same time keeping the scales of life balance.

Its okay to have fun, smile, play, laugh, and embrace the circle of life, as a matter of fact, we should encourage this in our life to the utmost. The universe within is so extraordinarily beautiful, and the mind is so rich and multifaceted, it's truly amazing how we can live a life span, yet we can be so alienated from it. From the beginning of psychology to present time psychologist have studied the mind and are still studying and learning it. Every empire, artifact, and ideology, was a thought before an intrinsic tangible, or an expressed whole. To attain richness, think like you are rich, and from this mindset, and way of thinking comes richness. Whatever you think in your heart, than so are you. And out of the heart are the issues of life. So if we do not become to consume with the inevitable of life, we can think it out, and work it out. We have to go through something, to get through something. Its nothing personal, nothing ventured, nothing gained. Having life experiences gives us our foundation to develop and fine tune our coping skills and our gifts. Think of it as your rites of passage. Whatever we encounter, experience, or struggle with, is a process for learning and development, and fine tuning our gifts, and character. Unless we are develop we will never be ripe. In other words, this is what makes us whole, and complete. The journey and discovery of life, and making modifications. Change is constant.

In order to build character, there is a prerequisite, so we will need a character test. In going to school what is the requirement to advance from a lower grade to a higher grade? There is a series of passing test. The same holds true in life. So life affords us this opportunity. Thank you life! It is an opportunity because it allows us to reach in, draw out, rise above, overcome, and evaluate ourselves, and take charge and control. We have to pass the test, and what makes a true believer is a true test. In order to have true confidence, you have to pass the confidence test, and it is nonnegotiable. With all problems in life, comes the opportunity for growth. Every life experience is an open invitation for growth. In retrospect we should be better off and not worse off. The more you overcome the more you become. Life does not owe any of us anything, so never foster this belief. Life is going to test each and every one of us. That's just the nature of life, and no one is exempt. We must use life the same way it uses us, and benefit in the process, and prosper to the limit. It has been said what does not kill us, makes us stronger and wiser. So give thanks to life for allowing us to reach our growth and potential. To many times we want to embrace the good in life, but are not willing to make the sacrifices. It has been said everybody wants to go to heaven, but nobody wants to die. Regardless to what we want in life, or out of life, we must give of our self. Throughout the process remain mindful, you may not be the person you desire at the moment, but with dignity feel good, because you are not the person you were. As a resurrected uninhibited life force pursue the opportunities of life, for now is the time to be encouraged. There is a time and moment for all things under the sun.

With a new lease on life, defuse from being bitter, and intensify being better. Being better will surely be reflective in one's daily living. No, longer should we remain active agents to our demise. We all at some point wanted a better job, more money, a business, or a specific goal, and for whatever reason we were crushed, or devastated when we fail short of the desired result. All of this was related to our mental frame of reference. Now being enlightened with a positive mental frame of reference, we can decipher in life, a better job, more money, or a specific goal isn't everyone's purpose. Nevertheless, we still bring value, need, and purpose to the planet. Whatever road of duty we travel in life provides us the opportunity to become more, and reach our potential. Regardless to what we were predestined to encounter in life, it is designed to make us stronger, wiser, and more knowledgeable. We are not born to remain idle and unexplored or unchallenged in life. Often when we are push around by life, we lose our faith and confidence, and then we live an idle existence, as opposed to being grateful. Sometimes it's the things we want most that we cannot handle. Then there are the times the best thing to happen to you is the worst thing that can happen to you. I have encountered people in life that had been fired and this forced them to start their own business, and as a result, they then had gained wealth and independence. Had they remained on their job they never would have had this level of success. I have read stories about how it appeared that some terrible things had happen to people, but in the aftermath of the experience, it was the best thing that ever had happen to them. One was of a lady in a marriage that wanted to start up a business, and had the vision to move forward with her inclination. But her husband did not share the same passion or vision. Therefore he was not supportive of her desires. As a result of them not sharing the same vision they ended up getting a divorce, and this had a painful effect on her. Emotionally the divorce had a hurtful impact on her. However, after time passed her wounds healed, and she had become a millionaire, as a result of her vision with her business. Then there was a story of a lady who had been married to her husband for more than twenty years, and she had never had a career other than being a housewife. Yet, one day her husband left her without a warning, and she was devastated and crushed. She had no training, no skills, and no employment background. Faced with what she thought was desperation she pleaded for her husband to come back and he refused. She felt betrayed, and used. She was confused, loss, and angry. Yet once she was able to get beyond the hurt and pain, she cleared her head, and started a business. This was the best thing that could have happen to her. When forced to be independent she looked to TLWI and discovered her inner self. This lead to her starting up a lucrative business. In these two situations, the worst thing that happen with these ladies were the best thing that could have happen to them. Use an obstacle as a challenge, or sign not to be denied. Use your problem solving skills to develop a plan of action and go forward. Another example, I recall a story of a woman who had peaked out in the workplace, and had reached the ceiling with her employer. There was no more room for advancement, unless she returned to college. So she tried enrolling in several colleges, but she was denied admission from each of them. After the experience of being denied college entry, she was right back at square root one. Being stuck in the workplace, and with no room for advancement. Feeling dejected, she stopped in town to have a cup of coffee, and just like in my experiences of meeting one person that gave me information to set my life on a new course, she encountered the same faith. She met a person, and shared her experience of the workplace with him, and he told her directly: if you are stuck start your own business. Those words stuck, and this is what propelled her to start up a successful business, and leave a limiting job. Life will find a way to help those seeking to help themselves. It just took receiving information from one person, the power of one, to lead her to TLWI, and this was enough incentive, and the inner self provided the drive. As I have said it is always the right time to get started, because help and assistance is wanting to help us through the aid of the universe. The universe is always conscious and waiting to extend help and champion people's cause. This is what it does, and it has always been this way and will always remain constant in its relationship with people. It has a helping nature.

Life is on our side, and we can do it. When you are actively in pursuit of a better way, life has no other choice, but to submit. I will never forget leaving the state of Texas and headed to the state of Minnesota with $160.00 dollars, and clueless to where I was going to stay. Soon as I arrived and got off the bus, I met and bonded with a homeless gentleman, and we went out for lunch. During lunch he directed me to a housing shelter. This allowed me to save my remaining $150.00. The Power of one and another angel sent to me.

Unbeknownst to me, upon arriving at the shelter, I discovered there was an employment vacancy for which I applied. The next day I was offered the position, and this position included housing and meals. I had negotiated one stipulation for terms of employment, and that being I would be granted two weeks to return to Texas to get my car, and then return. I then returned to Texas, and I was not convinced this was the place and direction to go. So I meditated and asked God for a sign, and I was directed to the library. When I arrived at the library, I went directly to the newspaper section, and checked out, three newspapers from other states. The Minneapolis newspaper being one of the three, and the first one I read. I had no idea what I was about to read, but it was a sign in the form of a story that I asked for. It was a story of a single mother with several children who was talking about how her relationship in Chicago was not healthy with her husband, and how he had abused her for the last time. So she decided to leave him, and everything she owned in Chicago. She was telling how she took the greyhound bus from Chicago to Minneapolis. And when she arrived in Minneapolis she secured housing, and was on public assistance of $620.00 dollars per month for a while, and she told how she had enrolled in trade school and completed her course. She was now employed as an electrician, and telling her story. Here was another angel that had been summoned to deliver a message for my taking. Likewise, here was the Power of One. I did not bother to read the other two papers.

Being inspired by this story with $200.00 dollars, I loaded up my car, and left Texas, and said Minneapolis Minnesota, here I come. After paying for gas, I arrived with a little over a hundred dollars, in a state, that I knew no one, but this would be the place to set my life on a positive course more than any place I have encountered. This is a place I went with a little over an hundred dollars, and knew no one, but my experience would evolve to parallel the lady's story from Chicago in the newspaper that I had read some 12 years prior.

Over and over again, I can account for if you take one step, life and the powers to be will direct you and help you. There is the saying to go on a long journey, the most important step is the first step. I wanted to play college football, and I did not have a scholarship, or the money to attend college, but I had a desire to play. I had no way of knowing how I was going to play, but still I found a way to play. Over the summer I loss 68 pounds got in shape and worked out every day. I knew I was going to play college football, and I did not know where, but I knew it was going to happen. Positive Thinking pays off. I targeted certain colleges, and when I got responses, I hitchhiked to them. I hitchhiked to several colleges that were in the range of 50 to hundred miles apart. After hitchhiking to one college, and after 6 rides later, and when I was dropped off, the driver asked me if I had any money? and I did not, so he gave me $20.00 dollars. The power of one, and once again another angel sent to me. The first day at this college, I met a student, and as we interacted we mention similar things, and unbeknownst to us, it turned out we were cousins. He then insisted I stay with him. For the duration of my campus visit, I had a place to stay, and food to eat. I even had a return trip home when I left. The fruits of my labor had paid off, after hitchhiking to several colleges, I had found a college to get in, and I made the team with a scholarship. I knew I was going to play college football, and I did. Once again life helps those that help themselves. And once again there was an angel waiting to aid me. As well, the universe connected me with rides, housing, food, money, and coaches to help manifest the desire of my heart to play college football.

Life is consistently busy and active, and is always ready to aid us and give us adversity at the same time. I had encountered divorce and had given up the house as requested by my ex-wife. Shortly afterwards I had filed for bankruptcy, so I had to take on apartment living. After living in the apartment for a year and half, I was ready to move into a house again, but with the challenges of rent, and child expensive it was next to impossible to save for a down payment. Well, I fasted and consoled God. I was told here is what you do. You are working two jobs, and that is all you need. What you do in six months after your lease expire, is sleep in your car for six months. That will eliminate debt, and create a money stream for you to have for your down payment. I had remembered from various sources of people who had become millionaires talk about the keys to acquiring wealth is having a job, saving your money, investing, and making sacrifices. I listen to the answer God had given me, and I slept in my car for six months. Came the end of July my lease was up. I went to work on my two jobs every day, never missed a day of work, never got sick, and applied the wealth principals and saved up $10, 000, and improved my credit score at the same time. No one knew I was homeless, or sleeping in my car. Came February 1st, 6 months to the day, and six months later, I moved into my 2500 square foot home. Out of no way came away. The mental training for life coupled with faith, being positive and being inner guided by TLWI and the universe prevailed once more.

Life will provide us the opportunity to be whole. As a favorite instructor of mine and clinical psychologist would say the goal of life, and the mission in life is to be whole. Seek and you shall find, look and you shall see, listen and you shall hear, knock and the door shall open. However, we have to operate from a frame of positive reference. Some person, some experience, a dream, a vision or premonition will introduce you to your life's work or calling. As a child I would have dreams about Minneapolis, Minnesota. All I remember about the dreams, were they were in an echoing repeated voice saying the words Minneapolis, Minnesota, Minneapolis, Minnesota, Minneapolis, Minnesota, and some twenty years forward and later, when I went and followed this dream, I said Minneapolis, Minnesota, here I come and there waiting for me was: housing, employment, and education. So as we plan, prepare and take action for our life we inherit a better understanding of success. We must be sincere, open, honest, and work diligently in our commitment to life.

Make everyday a holiday and each day find a moment to smile. Take one hour to relax your mind, body, and soul. Take the holistic approach to life. Let every worry and concern go, and find a total peace and quiet atmosphere. We cannot underscore the value of cleaning out the mind, and keeping it fine tuned. As we do this it is quality time with ourself. Before retiring for bed, think positive reassuring thoughts, and your expectancy of yourself. Record your goals and ideas on audio, and listen to them before bed, and again, once more in the morning. It is important to self-reflect, and reinforce positive thought patterns. We must be diligent in our commitment of life.

As we self-reflect and clean our mind, our affirmations can be as such: I commit to being positive, strong willed, healthy, wealthy, happy, hardworking, focus, discipline, in charge of my life, and master of my destiny. I refuse to be unproductive, unhappy, bitter, angry, guilt ridden, or guided by a negative spirit. I envision being the best example to myself, by the course of steady and consistent action I take. Also keep a chart of your goals, and ideas to be reviewed by your mind's eye daily. This keeps the information fresh in your mind, and at the same time, it keeps you mindful and focus.

Run your life like it is a successful business, and become business centered and business minded in relation to your life. There are few guarantees in life, and one of them is no one is going to be as loyal and supportive of your business as you. Do not expect the impossible. T.C.B. Take Care of your Business! And your life is your business, and it is personal. Master your circumstances and manage life affairs, the same way proprietors, partnerships, and corporations manage their business. Under the rules of management, or managing its not two sets of rules. In this case, one size fits all. Under the rules of managing it is not one rule for the capitalist, and another rule for the non-capitalist. The rule states to direct, control, or handle. We must direct, control, and handle our life. Every day we must apply these rules in our life for practical application. Lets use what I call the I.B.M chart for enrichment, and personal growth. This acronym is for Individual Business Manager. The Individual Business Manager chart 1-10 for storing and restoring life.

#1 What do I want to do in life?
#2 What are my assets, and liabilities? Take an inventory.
#3 Do some soul searching.
#4 Have a vision and expectancy of yourself.
#5 Maximize your potential.
#6 Come up with a plan of action, and then take action.
#7 Net worth with positive people.
#8 Practice being patient, because Rome wasn't built in a day.
#9 Have fortitude, because we will have to have mental flexibility.
#10 Be humble and glad about your I.B.M. status.

Throughout this book, there has been put emphasis on taking steps for action, the importance of working on self, and positive thinking, and being better and improved, by being led by TLWI. With our full pledge to being an Individual Business Manager: Stop! Pause! Exhale! And give yourself an applause, you've taken charge of your life. You, and only you are able to manifest TLWI.

In redirecting your life from inward, look at the attributes, and adjectives that were revealed about your character. For an improved lifestyle requires being a self-starter and doer. It takes courage to examine and take charge of your life, and being willing to fail or succeed. Courage allows us to be persistent, unique, different, flexible, and to see a way out of no way. It takes courage to confess, I'd like more and better in life, but I don't know where to begin. The answer is always with self. Inward then outward. Courage galvanizes us to be bold, and when you are bold, you deal with issues to get solutions. Being bold is your personal ritual to be enthusiastic, daring, fearless, and determine. You will not stop demanding a better life for yourself, and you will not take no as an answer. Every time you hear the word no out of context, transpose the letters. No transpose is on. That is the hint to get on with your life, and move on to the bigger and better. Boldness won't allow you to stop, your slogan will be can't stop, won't stop until I reach the top. This means you are going to have to put in work. Taking initiative, with the presence of mind to take action and be productive enables us to enjoy the fruits of our labor.

All along, we have been equipped with courage, initiative, boldness, and inner leadership qualities. Yet we have been outer sink with these qualities, and this is contrary to our nature. We were created to be at harmony within, but lack of positive thinking has disconnected us from this course. Now we are placed back on a harmonious course of positive and rightful thinking. When we are reposition in life, we can live in sync with our inner self; therefore, we love ourself wholeheartly and unconditionally, and this love is at the essence of our core. On this quest of living through inner leadership, and positive thinking we live without settling or placing limits in our mind due to negative thinking. Again, not settling leads to action, and when we take action we get action. Simple mathematics, something plus something = more something, nothing + nothing= nothing, and nothing leads to negative thinking, and hardships, and despair in life.

There is a story in the bible of three men each given a certain amount of talents. One five talents, one two talents, and the other one talent. The men given five and two talents worked and increased their talents, but the man given one talent buried his. When payday came, the men who worked and increased their talents were multiplied and increased in their blessing. Blessings are rewards, and treasures and are wonderful gifts of reality. A blessing of increase means there is no depth, and it can be beyond measure. Now on the other hand, the ungrateful man who was dissatisfied, and given one talent, he buried it. He simply said forget it, and he did not put in any labor or work. Instead of increasing what he was entrusted with, he basically chose to do nothing. So according to his effort, and work, when it was time for his reward, he was paid according to his labor and work. His effort justified his outcome. He was cursed and stripped of his talent. That is what a lot of us do, we bury our talent. If we are not given an ideal situation, or a convenient situation we simply abandon ship. We say forget it, and basically do nothing. We are dissatisfied and full of resentment. Then we use many invalid excuses to justify our lack of commitment, and essentially we bury our talent. How often have we heard it expressed or even expressed it ourselves? I just can't, I would but, someday I will, I tried but, you just don't understand, it is too hard, so we do nothing other than complain. Reframe from this way of thinking and abandon it. It means us no good. Anything that means you no good, keep it out of your spirit. Cant isn't an option. Furthermore, can't lives on Wont Street. In truth these are the curses you are placing in your life. You are being rewarded according to your negative thinking, and your labor, or lack of labor or effort, or lack of effort. In addition, when you're striding for excellence from within, you're more concern about what you can do, so you operate on this principle, which is the principle of can do.

Be an inspiration for someone to model and emulate, be the standard barrier, you can do it. Do what? You'll decide that. Because remember anything that has been done, or needs to be done, or will be done has a common theme. Which is: It was all the product of a live breathing person that has the same origin as us all. Therefore, we all can claim that vast biological fact, and intelligence base. Said another way, we are all one in the circle of life. So Wake Up! Open Up! and Stand Up! Be an active spirit, and a living energy force, because the way to happiness and freedom is clear. Today is the first day of the rest of my life. It starts now, so say and believe it, and feel it. I feel good, I feel strong, I feel inspired, I feel rejuvenated, I feel great, I've expanded my knowledge base, and I truly feel empowered. Life is wonderful and I feel good with my choices. I'm doing more, I'm pursing positive and meaningful goals in my life. I am my future, I refuse to sell myself short, I refuse to be depress, I refuse to be the champion of negative thinking, and I refuse to stunt my growth. Though I will accept constructive criticism and repair my life as needed, in no way, shape, or form will I resent the person I was born to be. Today and every day, I am striding to be the best me humanly possible. I take full responsibility, knowing I'm responsible for my success, or lack of success.

Key workable components of TLWI are grounded in the workable solutions of being a self-help specialist. Physician Heal Thy Self as it is written in scripture. Therefore we must come up with a life plan, and lay the ground work and format to maximize our potential. Examples would be square away any stressful circumstance in your life that mean you no good. If you owe someone pay them, or make amends to make the wrong right. If you have to attend credit workshops, or get credit counseling, or get information from books or the web than do what you have to. I was able to circumvent several thousands of dollars of debt from reading books. Having bad credit was a good experience, and the experience taught me a lot. As I have mentioned sometime the best thing that can happen to you, is the worst thing that can happen to you. I read books on various debt situations, and attended many credit workshops. I have read books on alternative and creative ways to save money. This information still holds true, and serves me well today. If I never would have had delinquent credit status, I never would have been inspired, and motivated to seek out this information. In the long haul it has saved me vast sums of money. Knowledge is power. It has been said: The more you learn, the more you earn, and learning is tied to health, wealth, happiness, and savings and holistic living. So as a result of me being in debt, I have been rewarded tenfold, now I can make better inform decisions about credit and money matters.

Imagine being inform and knowledgeable on business matters which will consequently allow you to enter mutual encounters of win/win. The rewards you reap will be enormous, and are not limited to the following: monetary, stress reduction, increased energy, keener thinking, quality time for love ones, a boost in self-confidence, and overall peace of mind. When you enter new avenues of your life you have never explored, there are major rewards and benefits there just waiting for you to claim them, and in claiming them, you will represent yourself to the utmost in every aspect of your life. Repeatedly, you'll reap the rewards. You'll save in spending; you get the best rates on buying homes and cars. Truly, your life encounters will be win/win. I recall being in the market place for a home and talking to a realtor, and being assured his extended offer couldn't and wouldn't be beat. Because I had bad credit, I had read books on credit problems, and had read about a flexible seller, and contract for deed, and sandwich release options. In short, I knew I had options, and if nothing else, I had required knowledge from my research, which had revealed to me: do not like a house so much you cannot say no to it, or do not borrow trouble. I therefore relied on the information that I had attained as a result of my adverse credit, and I tapped into this history, of researching the market place. In the end I was not only able to top his couldn't beat, wouldn't beat offer, I beat it by 35% less. Having bad credit was a blessing in disguise, and I'm grateful to this day for the experience of it. It propelled me to research the market place, and now if I am unsure of any life encounter, I will research the market place. Case and Point: I was in an automobile accident, and I researched the market place, bought a book on how to write demand letters, how to organize the information, and the rules of negotiating settlements. I learned about the insurance damage formula, soft tissues injuries, and how writing a few letters, and making a few phone calls can enable you to represent yourself. Further I learned how to prove your case. It went on to give information about how you know your injuries, losses, and damages better than anyone else. Therefore, if you follow the process, you can represent yourself. I used this book and received a $23,500 settlement. Life and the universe helps those that help themselves.

The good things about the laws that govern the universe are: they will submit to any person that works them. Everything under the sun and in the universe is governed by laws. There is the of law reproduction, the law of nature, there are wealth laws, there are spiritual laws, and there are the seven laws of the universe. Two I will expound on, one being The Law of Cause and Effect, and the other The Law of Polarity. "First The Law of cause and effect which states that for every action, there is an equal and opposite reaction. Every cause has an effect, and every effect has a cause. Be at cause for what you desire, and you will get the effect. All thought is creative, so be careful what you wish for . . . you will get it. How to apply it: Consistently think and act on what you desire to be effective at getting it." Secondly," The Law of polarity states that everything has an opposite. Hot-Cold, Light-Dark, Up-Down, Good-Bad. In the absence of that which you are not, that which you are . . . is not. Polar opposites make existence possible. If what you are not didn't coexist with what you are, then what you are could not be. Therefore, do not condemn or criticize what you are not or what you don't want. How to apply it: Look for the good in people and situations. What you focus on, you make bigger in your life." We are an outer and inward world govern by laws. This is why it is important to have the proper mindset, because whatever we send out in the universe it will come right come back to us. This is called Karma. This is critical because we attract and pull to us what is in the universe of our mind. This is also one of the seven laws called Law of Attraction. Over and over again, the universe has aided me. For taking action: I have received 3 degrees that I never planned for, and all of them were attain without sorrow. I have received thousands of dollars just by writing letters, I have been showed how to use my resources to save thousands of dollars, I have moved to several states within the United States without knowing anyone, or without having any education and with no more than $ 200.00 dollars in my pocket or no money in the bank. Further, I have been able to play college football despite not having any resources other than a desire and positive attitude to do it. In addition, this included going to the country of Colombia with $ 400.00 dollars, and not having a place to stay, or not being able to speak spanish. Still the same, I secured housing, and food for four days, and left with $125.00.

Throughout life, I have encountered, where there is a will there is a way, and when you take action, you get action. I know without question, what you put into life is what you get out of life. Information will find you and stick to you like a magnet. It can come in the form of a book, a person, an experience, technology, or a dream. The range is enormous, and vast and wide of gaining knowledge and information that will put your life on a new and heighten platform. First we must have the proper positive mindset, and the inner leadership of TLWI. A whole new world will open up to you. I recall befriending a college instructor and clinical psychologist who I had kept in touch with for ten years, and who was a trusted leader, guide and mentor. This professor and I would engage in a wide range of topics over the years, in the field of psychology, humanities, and life. He would share his profound knowledge base with me that he had received from his practice, and his study, and experiences. At the time, I never knew the value of what this beloved man was imparting in me. Further, I never realized how the universe had sent another angel in my life, and for ten years he instilled wise wisdom within me. He has been a credit to much of my success in life, and much of his wisdom is reflected in this book. The Power of One. Life helps those that help themselves.

The power of faith and action is a strong weapon. When you operate on this level the floodgates of thoughts will overtake you with positive ideas, and positive thought patterns. With me this has included exploring the fields of dietary laws and the fields of nutrition.

When I took action in this area of my life I lost 70 pounds. I decided to implement a dietary law into my life. My goal was to strengthen my immune system, clean my colon, flush out my system, and include energy and brain foods in my diet. This would include implementing the proper nutrition and balance of water, proteins, carbohydrates, fats, and fiber into my body that would enhance it, and not abuse it. We are what we eat mentally and physically. In transforming my eating habits my whole focus and outlook had changed. I didn't want any deficiencies present in my body, so this had a ripple effect that lead me to detoxing my body of free radicals, and pollutants. The floodgate of ideas has an overall trickledown effect of producing overall healthy living. These are life experiences I share, because I know we all are capable of taking personal action to improve our life, and then reaching back to aide others. Positive thinking, faith and taking action, and embracing the inward leadership from TLWI will lead to a life of inward and outward happiness. This is the holistic balance we will reap. We are made from the inside out. This way of thinking draws the positive sources to you. I wanted to write a book. Therefore I put my focus on this subject, and I did not know where to begin. I went to the book store, and the information was right in a book, as if it had my name on it. The information was: Write a few pages a day for a certain amount of time, and before you know it, you will have wrote a book. This was followed by another book I read which shared: market yourself and put together a press kit. Further, I was listening to a great writer tell her story on keys to being a writer. She talked about how you need to get out and see the world, so you will have a broad perspective. I took those words to heart. Futhermore, I would read a book about a famous television talk show host tell how he basically did the same thing. Which was he toured the country to get a broad perspective of things. Replicated success.

I begin touring the country from state to state calling this tour operation mental training. I partook in homeless shelters, soup lines, bonding and uniting with the homeless, attending seminars, workshop programs, and a variety of spiritual worship ceremonies. These were enhancing and rewarding experiences, and at the same time, it supported my aim of getting my Liberal Arts Degree of being wide in scope, in which I was clueless at the time, but once again life helps those that help themselves. One of my most endearing moments was in talking with a homeless gentleman from Washington DC, who imparted to me if you don't know what to do with money, you shouldn't spend it. Sound Information! Then there were the two inspiring men from Oakland, California who inspired me to live regardless. Not so much by blowing their horn, but by their deeds, and action. These men resided as vagabonds and drifted from park to park, and abandon building to abandon building. Despite this they were able to hold down jobs, and attend college, and read the newspaper every day. What was impressive was these men were well informed on current events, and enlighten on the depth of life. Then there was the strength and brevity of the twenty-three year old single mother of 3, and who was living in public housing in Las Vegas, Nevada whom to this day, had the best smile I've encountered. The power of a smiling face. She held it together well. I'm eternally grateful to the millionaire that I met from Alvin, Texas who told me a poor man should take a rich man out to lunch. I'll always be thankful to the recovering drug addict and professional musician from Buffalo, NY, that was up early every morning and full of energy, and ready to work on his dream of continuing his music, and who told me you never know who's among you. I will always cherish what the commissioner from Florida told me in telling me to read 3,650 pages per year, but do it at a pace of ten pagers per day, for one year. This equates to starting out at a small series of goals to finish one big goal. Then there was the counselor from Idaho who told me all people are worthy of trust, just on different levels, and its up to you to figure out on what level. I will never forget what the imprisoned and convicted murder and business owner told me. In business you will have to be able to read the three kind of people you will encounter. One type is the one who can help you, one is the type that can hurt you, and the other is the type that cant help or hurt you. But you'll need to access the situation within five minutes so it will not be a hindrance to your goal. I'll always be mindful to the training director of the department of corrections for his imparted wisdom in sharing with me he'll believe even a lair if he knows the truth and hear the truth. All of these examples and encounters are from people from all walks of life. That has been positive in scope in my growth and development.

In addition, to touring the country and getting different perspectives from people from all walks of life, I wanted to offer an extended helping hand to the under privilege, and marginalized in society. My goal was to work as a volunteer in the prisons, but the opportunity presented itself in the terms of employment, so I took the job with the intent of enhancing and expanding my knowledge base to help work with downtrodden people. Some of my most endearing experiences in life were when I could communion, and be as one and entrusted with convicts and inmates' innermost secrets. I had the pleasure of interviewing them on criminal and crime issues. Topics were wide in scope ranging from rape, biker gangs, substance abuse, drug addiction, child molestation, gangs, gang violence, gang rules, religion, homicide, capital punishment, death row, and poverty to mention some. It didn't stop here. I interviewed the warden, and at his direction, I took a course at the local television cable company. I then branched out doing more interviews on college campuses, political and social events. This was my source to broaden my mind to help stimulate my writing skills. This is from a person that was born with a slur of speech and not able to talk until I was five.

I recall visiting the country of Colombia and being among the local natives. They were very impoverished in terms of living conditions and economics, but among their mannerism I could never tell. I witnessed families of 6 and 7 living in one or two rooms, and people sleeping in cracks of buildings, in and under trees, some walking the streets day and night with nowhere to go, and children as young as six getting up at 4 or 5 in the morning getting ready to start working and hustling to make money, just to have a meal for the day, but they had a positive state of mind. I've consulted many sources profited from them all, and this is an option available for each and every one of us. We can profit and benefit to the limit from the many sources of life. Life is the many inter connective sources both good and bad that bind us together for the common good. Life is not about me and you, I, we, and us without regard for the whole. We are all interconnected, and no one person is an island. A leader cant be a leader without a follower, a teacher cant be a teacher without a student, a doctor cant be a doctor without a patient, a winner cant be a winner without a loser, a lawyer cant be a lawyer without a client, and a buyer cant be a buyer without a seller. So in putting primary emphasis on our deeds and actions, we cannot diminish or under emphasize the importance of connecting with others. We are all one.

Theres a story of a father and son where the father asks the son to move a stack of wood, and do his best in the process. The son moved the entire stack except for one piece which was too heavy. So the son told his father I'm done moving the stack of wood except for one heavy piece of wood. The father responded son did you do your best like I asked? Yes sir responded the son. I did my very best. The father then asked, well if you did your very best, why didn't you ask for help? The son simply over looked the importance of connecting with his father for help. The father enlighten the son with a valuable lesson, it's no crime to ask for help. The moral is though we look inward first for leadership, we must not overlook the outward need for help.

I have heard many famous people talk about the importance of people. People make the world go round. People are the most important, and valuable resource on the planet. I have read where in business profit and product is of high priority, but of greater priority are people. Regardless of what language you speak people come first. I will put it like this, first comes people, then 2nd comes people, and then 3rd comes people, and then all other things. Assuredly by putting people first, and following the instructions of being your own physician, and Individual Business Manager, this synthesis will trickle down to every aspect of your life; therefore, every aspect of your life will improve. Relationships will improve, stress decreases, energy levels will expand and increase, and you will have freedom, and control in your life, independence and personal power will have practical meaning. You will not only see the light, but you will be the light.

In becoming self-actualize and whole, you become a better decision maker, and this could be the difference in marriage or divorce, leading or following, hell or heaven. You become a better planner, this is the difference between living beyond your means, owning your own business, being self-sufficient, having a savings for a rainy day, renting or buying a house or owning your house, being dependent, or Independent. We reap the positive benefits of growth and Positive Thinking.

With growth comes responsibility, growth is like an introductory course to put us on the path for knowledge, wisdom, and understanding. Which allows us to integrate our accumulation of thoughts, ideas, concepts, beliefs, and experiences for a meaningful and enhanced life. Isn't it the true purpose of education, knowledge, wisdom, and understanding to liberate, unify, empower, and put us at peace with no regard for race, color, creed, sex, or status?

Taking a step in the right direction is critical, because in order to go far you must begin near and the most important step is the first one. There is an adage that says every expert was once a beginner at something. It is okay to take the first step, and it is okay to be a beginner, just look at what company you join. You will win some, and fall short on some, but it is okay, because a winner will overcome the circumstances of life. Winners will do their best, and if they do not get their desired goal, then they make modifications, and move full steam ahead. They refuse to lose. I'm partial to the slogan there are no losers. Yet, there is what I call volunteer losers, professional complainers, someone who is always sick, someone who is always depressed, someone who is always in turmoil, or at odds with life, or anything in general. But in reality, they are the primary agent of their lamenting, and turmoil based on their state of negative mind, and life choices. We all can identify with people like this. They are what I call the victim syndrome at heart. Yet the beauty in this is we can exercise our power of choice to reconcile any adverse relationship.

I think there are three types of reality:

Reality #1. It is what it is.

Reality #2. Is negative perception reality, this category of people comes up with every conceivable excuse, or explanation to justify why they aren't doing something, or why they cant do something. In reality their position has no merit, and is a fallacy tied to their state of mind, to support their claim. They have put their belief into practice. This is the agent that has robbed them in life of happiness and their constant wellbeing. Emancipate yourself from the dream killer of negative thinking.

Reality #3. This is what I call positive perception reality. An example would be you set a goal for yourself, and you envision doing it, and you do it, no questions asked. It's a done deal. The spirit of being led by the power of positive thinking and TLWI.

In closing develop yourself, know yourself, look inward, and know the depth of your inward character, and characteristics, and attributes of a natural born leader, that is waiting to be tapped into, and released. Know that inward there is a teacher, leader, guide, and IBM. Be your own leader, because within every person resides The Leader Within.

Printed in the United States
By Bookmasters